M000032177

Ravishing Pearl

Poetry by

Rita Conestabile

Copyright © 2020 by Rita Conestabile

All rights reserved.

ISBN 978-1-62806-315-8 (print | paperback)
ISBN 978-1-62806-316-5 (print | hardback)

Library of Congress Control Number 2021907687

Published by Salt Water Media
29 Broad Street, Suite 104
Berlin, MD 21811
www.saltwatermedia.com

Graphic cover design by Beatrice Sims

All images are courtesy of Canva except the following: photographer credit goes to Laurie Ruggiero for the author photo and photos on pages 20 and 31; photographer credit goes to Rita Conestabile for photos on pages 31, 75 (top), 101, 131, 156, and 183; photographer credit goes to Jason D'Amore for the photo on page 60; photographer credit goes to Paulina McCoy for photos on pages 68, 112, and 216; and photographer credit goes to Larry Peck for the photo on page 120.

Ravishing Pearl

Acknowledgements

Thanks to all my extended family and friends around the world,
No matter the distance - you're *always* in my heart...

Special thanks to my sisters,
Anne Marie Conestabile and **Antoinette Nazar**

Daughter-in-law, **Pauline Peck**

Future daughter-in-law, **Mallory Brown**

My other daughter, **Paulina McCoy**

And to the newest addition in my family,
now and forever in my heart,
My grandson, **Marcus Lorenzo Peck**

Additional thanks to:
The **ADVERSARIES** I've encountered in my life...
Without you, my strength and perseverance
wouldn't be *half* of what it is...

And to a very special person,
who has proven that not all angels in our midst wear wings...

Dedication

For *Max*, *Sean* and *Rachel*

I *always* knew the day would come
Since my earliest dreams
When I was so young
Imagining your faces
And who you were destined to be
From the miracle of one
Then eventually three
Two boys, and a girl
Who came into my life
And *forever* changed my world...

For My Parents...

Giovanni and Romana Conestabile

Whose love for each other

Created me

Table of Contents

Poems

Like a delicate flower
Sleeping throughout the night
The *awakening* begins...
Each of her petals open
For dawns sensual light
Casting shadows
Where lover's dream
The nightbird sings the movement
Of the joyous river stream
Drifting harmoniously
Through thick and thin
Until the day is over
And nightfall begins

- The Awakening -
Rita Conestabile

He said she was dark and beautiful
He was reminded
Of her poetry, her music
And her rebellious nature
With a love for artistic boys
She always knew
This was after all
Most certain
And *painfully* true

- Dark and Beautiful -
Rita Conestabile

I dream of you
But I still don't know your name
I know that when we meet
I'll *never* be the same
I treasure the thought
Of being together at last
Erasing all memories
Of the tumultuous past
Here and now
All hurting is done
Eternity begins when
We are one

- To Whom It May Concern -
Rita Conestabile

I've loved you
Every step of the way
But never more
Than I do today...

- Every Step of the Way -
Rita Conestabile

I long to dwell
In the sensual world
Surrounded with lavender
Crushed velvet and cascading pearls
Where roses take pride
In each thorn they display
Accepting their differences
They show us the way
Even time has chosen its favorite spot
In the hidden field of memories
Amongst beautiful lilies
And forget me nots
With wild abandon, I'll meet you there
To dance and dream without a care

- Sensual World -
Rita Conestabile

In lieu of you, I *will not* do...

- In Lieu of You -
Rita Conestabile

Be the women
Uncompromised
By the dictates of society
Let them think of you
What they will
Let your anthem be the
Truth
And may you continue
To *speak* it
Until time stands still

- Uncompromised -
Rita Conestabile

Dreams overcome
The sadness we endure
When hope leads the way
Love is the cure...

- Dreams Overcome -
Rita Conestabile

Inevitably, he would wear black
And just one look from his celestial eyes
Could bring to life the entire universe
Of the night sky
Blazing meteors at the touch of his skin
Swirling nebulae
Where his body ends, and mine begins
Even Aurora Borealis
More brilliant than ever
Had finally met her match
Displaying an envious shade of luminous
Green
Knowing we were *so much* more
Than she had ever seen

- Celestial Eyes -
Rita Conestabile

I often say, "I can't imagine"
Yet I always do... I *feel* the pain
That you've been through

- I Often Say -
Rita Conestabile

More than ever
All she really wanted
Was to live
To feel every moment
With eyes wide open
And a heart full of love to give
To peel away the blisters
Allowing the necessary bleed
To heal, feel, and to finally
Be completely ok
With it all

- More Than Ever -
Rita Conestabile

When Love happens
Your soul releases
- A burst of *forever*-
Disguised as stars
In the night sky

- **Forever** -
Rita Conestabile

My strength
Wasn't born, on easy street...

- My Strength -
Rita Conestabile

Let's write a dream
We'll call it our song
It's the music we'll hear
Our whole life long
A choir of angels
For each of us sings
From the moment of birth
As we breathe our life in
Though clouds may appear
We'll rejoice just the same
When the father comes calling
Each one of us by name

- Let's Write A Dream -
Rita Conestabile

I've spent a lifetime
In a single day
Dreaming about tomorrow
As if it were
Here today

- I've Spent A Lifetime -
Rita Conestabile

The prelude begins
Escape to this sacred ground
Rest upon the place
Where the symphony resounds
Once you're there you'll realize
She is the most beautiful music
You will ever hear
Exclusively reserved
For your eyes
Your lips
Your ears

- The Prelude -
Rita Conestabile

Like sparrows uncertain
Perched on the water's edge
We balance between
The beginning
The middle
And the end

- Sparrows -
Rita Conestabile

Having endured its loss so many times
I wonder if it shall ever remain
If given the chance to bask there so deeply
In love again
With lips as soft as rose petal dew
I speak your name
Though I still haven't met you
I know you're there
But *where* do you exist?
This force between us
Is unbearable to resist

- Having Endured -
Rita Conestabile

Heartbeats can be heard
Without a single word
If you'd only *listen*...

- Heartbeat -
Rita Conestabile

A thousand light years
From now
The moon will echo
The love she breathed into
The universe
And when you *feel* it
Stardust will enter
Your soul...

- **Light Years** -
Rita Conestabile

Once you cross over the line
Of a painful end
The same magnetic lure
Doesn't work
To pull you back to try again
You finally realize your self-worth
And to compromise
In that department, just *isn't* an option
Anymore

- The Line -
Rita Conestabile

Encounter love
In all its glorious ways
A lifelong journey
Whose path
We often stray
When hearts take the lead
The perils are real
Stay focused - be true
Love all that is given
In the name of *love*
For you...

- Encounter Love -
Rita Conestabile

Walking on eggshells
Isn't how it's supposed to be
Being trampled in your garden
Was nothing new to me
You challenged me
To the point of no return
Oh, how I wanted to stay
And sing the praises
Of true love everlasting
But silence prevailed
And *muted* every note
Of our love song

- **Eggshells** -
Rita Conestabile

Part of her wanted to die
But the rest of her *wouldn't* give in
Even when the music stopped
She continued to sing
Sadly, he didn't hear a word she said
She continued to smile
While her heart still bled

- Part of Her -
Rita Conestabile

Breathe with me once again
Be the air that circulates my soul
Be the season of desire that *never* gets cold
So that we may sleep in peace, when we are old
Blow your kisses to the gentle waves of the wind
Without hesitation
I will wait
With doors wide open
To let you in...

- I Will Wait -
Rita Conestabile

Rise and Shine my darling girl
Run with the wind my precious pearl
Hear our song when it rains
As each storm passes release your pain
Kiss the moon
Be wild and free
As in my heart
You will *always* be

- Rise and Shine -
Rita Conestabile

Words cluster in her mind
like overgrown fields of poppies
Covering the landscape while she sleeps
Always speaking to her in the language of love
Pollinating thoughts, strewn about
Consistently multiplying even at 3 am
Synchronizing themselves with the rise of the moon
As it reaches its nocturnal peak
They seem to share an insatiable desire
To make their presence known to her
Before they slip away
Acting as if they'd *never* return again
To see the light of day

- **Nocturnal Peak** -
Rita Conestabile

Peace still grows...
Where love once
Bloomed

- Peace -
Rita Conestabile

Half way 'round the world
She stands on a beach - smiling
Her eyes sparkle
I imagine streaks of glimmering shades
Of dusty blond - hiding
In her loosely woven braids, blowing freely
In the wind
While I on the other hand
hold on tightly to my cup of tea
My one and only solace
In this solitary confinement
That continues to separate
You from me

- Facebook Friend -
Rita Conestabile

Like a shooting star across the sky
Life comes and goes in the *blink* of an eye
While you're here continue to shine
And be at peace with what you do
With loves everlasting light – burning so bright
It'll have no choice but to illuminate you

- Shooting Star -
Rita Conestabile

Having lost all direction
He said my curves were his compass
His heart and soul were my salvation
Our lips our only navigation
My scent, touch and taste
Were his consolation for living
I was his destination
And when he found me
He *knew* he was home

- Compass -
Rita Conestabile

Earthly numbers don't always add up
When you are given a heavenly decree
Here we think one and one makes two
But when God is in our midst
You and I make three

- **Earthly Numbers** -
Rita Conestabile

Poetry filters pain
The two are allies
In a constant state of smoldering flames
Beware my companion
Of passions *devious* flares
Lest we succumb to its inevitable despair
It's love and hallowed ground we seek to find
But in this inferno we lose our mind

- Poetry Filters Pain -
Rita Conestabile

My favorite part of me
Is *you*...

- You -
Rita Conestabile

I am self-contained
In the embodiment of my skin
Keeping to myself
Seldom letting anybody in
Yet, like a war - torn comrade
Who'll *always* have your back
Watch the bloodhounds rise
If someone I love is under attack
The jugular and I have met before
I'm not afraid to open that door
Yet a world of peace lies within
Beneath the olive complexion
Of this Italian skin

- **Skin** -
Rita Conestabile

Dear Queen of Sheba
You are *so much less*
Than I thought you were
Your beauty is now faded
To nothing but a *blur*

- **Queen of Sheba** -
Rita Conestabile

Little does he know
That the sea of glass beneath his feet
With all those jagged edges
Are the remaining pieces
Of the broken heart that's left of you
A beautiful mosaic, that he once knew
But now
And long after you've been gone
Shards of you will continue to pierce his skin
And from this day forward
He will instinctively watch his every step

- Shattered Mosaic -
Rita Conestabile

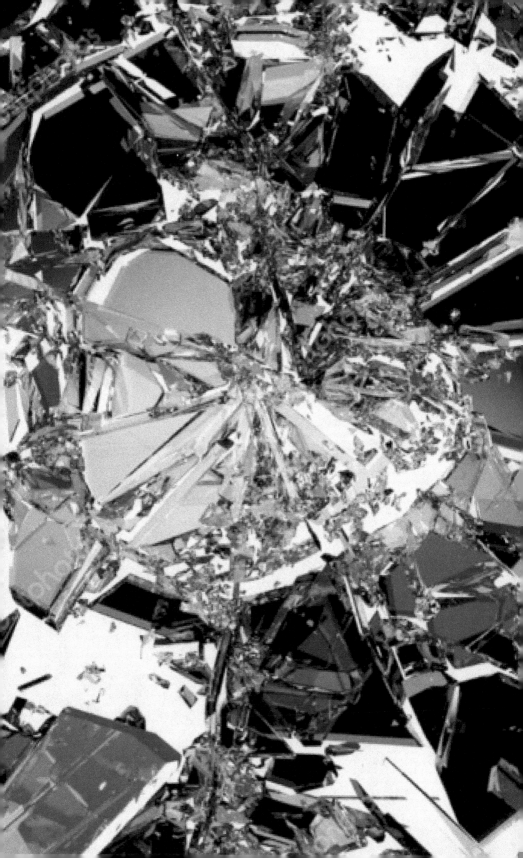

Formal education, or the lack thereof
Should not stop us
From expanding the depths of our humanity
We live, we breathe, and someday we'll die
This is all the knowledge we need
To positively impact the world we inhabit
And in turn
Our own souls accordingly

- **Formal Education** -
Rita Conestabile

There is so much more
To be seen of her
Restless is the mind
Of an artistic girl
Weaving her words
Or perfecting a hue
Creating her magic
To satisfy you
So very pleasing to your soul
You proceed to let her light in
But tangled in the chaos of her beauty
No one ever wins
Yet alone in her glow
Even time stands still
You've always loved this girl
And somehow she knows
You always will

- Artistic Girl -
Rita Conestabile

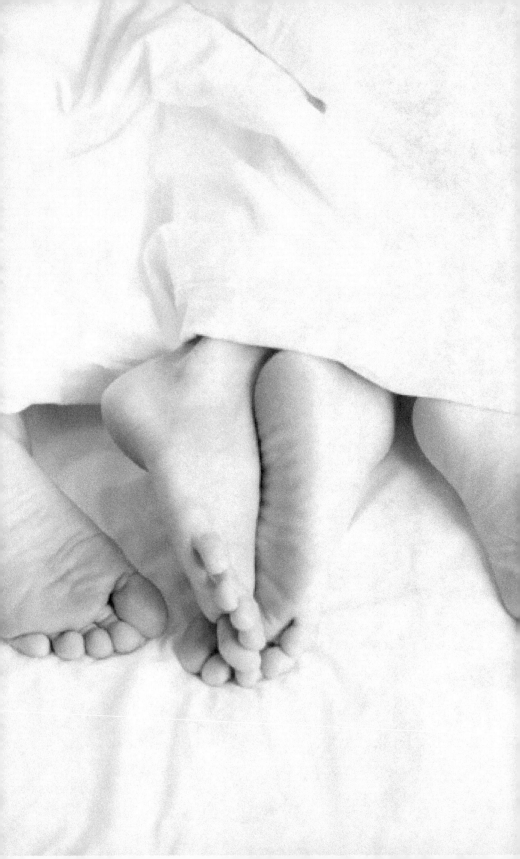

At the foot of the bed
Is where they meet
Below the blankets with their feet
No need for talk or explanation
The time has come
For *sole* communication

- **Sole Communication** -
Rita Conestabile

When you are lying next to me
All I want to feel is your sweet serenity
In this moment of time
You are my everything, so perfectly aligned
Depths revealed, truths explored
Compassionate heart, I so adore
Longing, anticipation - culminated exclamation
Again, again and again
I shall forever embrace, this treasured vision
That time *cannot* erase

- Sweet Serenity -
Rita Conestabile

LOVE:

Know it
Sow it
Grow it

- Love -
Rita Conestabile

Be the *wildcard* of your destiny
And play your hand
Accordingly

- Wildcard -
Rita Conestabile

You are my morning habit
And my nighttime fix
I surrender the day
To your goodnight kiss
Though words do charm
They often obscure
Loves true calling
For only *Love* will endure

- Morning Habit -
Rita Conestabile

The most *beautiful* place
You will ever be
Is inside your mother's heart

- Beautiful Place -
Rita Conestabile

I'm so amazed
By the stars in the sky
The prelude to creation
Before mankind
Yet, cosmic is the dust
That created our minds
Swirling and twirling, since the beginning of time
I am - you are
We shall, forever be...

- Amazed -
Rita Conestabile

I give her a wink
She gives me a nod
My girlfriend and me
Two peas in a pod

- Peas In A Pod -
Rita Conestabile

I am a magnet, drawn to the center core
Of life's endless meanderings of her seaside shores
Frothy white caps, with exhilarating appeal
Rejuvenation to my body, to my soul it heals
Blue angel sky, white powder sand
Caressing my fingers, as it slips through my hands
Ageless and timeless, in this beauty surreal
Like a giggling child, is how I feel
Creating my own language, rhythm and rhyme
Here in this *Para-Dizzial* Island
I find so sublime

- Magnet -
Rita Conestabile

Live *passionately* – Love *Profoundly*

- Live Passionately – Love Profoundly -
Rita Conestabile

She catapulted herself onto the horizon
From there
She could touch the sky
With baby's breath and angel wings
Her hopes and dreams
Learned to *fly*

- Horizon -
Rita Conestabile

Be at peace my love
Dream of me
The heavens are wide open
For all the world to see
Be at peace my love
May your heart be worry free
Together is our season
For all eternity

- Be At Peace -
Rita Conestabile

Waves come and go
In their rhythmic flow
Like a serenade in the moonlight
Underneath stars aglow
She has lost herself there
Many time before
Her spirit drifting
Through every open door
What seems surreal
Is in fact truth these days
Alone in her wandering mind
Trying to unravel this twisted maze
Though darkness stretches across the wasteland
She accepts the comfort
Of a compassionate hand
The sun rays rival her despair
While the sea offers cleansing
As she breaths deep, the salt in the air
Little by little, a new star is born
To illuminate her soul, while she's here
And *long after* she is gone

- **Waves** -
Rita Conestabile

Twilight awakens
Her deepest slumber
While *he* takes a bow
She takes a number

- Twilight -
Rita Conestabile

The sweetest of words bestowed upon me
Is that of, *Mother*
Exclusively reserved for my beloved three
Our journey in life, a continuously evolving tale
No matter the hardships
Our love will continue without fail
Though our paths may lead us to live separately
Our roots remain *united*, in our family tree

- **Sweetest Words** -
Rita Conestabile

Blended harmoniously
With a myriad of colors
Brushstrokes drenched in patriotism
Mixed with the heroic flair of bloodshed hands
The image it portrays is clear
For those who have taken the stand
United in sacrifice, for our sake and our land
Comradery is the medium
Apparent on this canvas wall
Absorbed are the stains of the fallen
Muted with our tears, as we recall
Gratitude prevails - we salute with pride
Our spirits are lifted as we raise the flag high
One nation under God
Born on the fourth of July

- Fourth of July -
Rita Conestabile

Look for *kindness*
It doesn't have an expiration...
Even if the package is damaged

- Look for Kindness -
Rita Conestabile

Outside my window
Thoughts are falling from the sky
I see them clearly but not with my eyes
Descending in rhythm these moments in time
Swirling like leaves embracing my mind
Strands of silver in sunlight gleam
Embracing the view of my window dream
The lovely peacock stands on guard
Chiming so sweetly from my backyard
With awe and wonder, I dare not seek
To repair heaven's faucet
Where falling thoughts leak

- Falling Thoughts Leak -
Rita Conestabile

Tumultuous is our life
When even the *wind*
Seeks shelter
From the impending storm

- Tumultuous Is Our Live -
Rita Conestabile

Most of my time
Is never really my own
So I run away
Don't mind being alone
What more can I say?
Revolving doors suit me just fine
Lock me in
I lose my mind

- Revolving Doors -
Rita Conestabile

The distant sun
Made its decent behind the mountain
Melting into the landscape
As it dipped into the horizon
She swore off falling for a mirage
That so many of us continue to see
But there he was, on his high horse
Standing right in front of me
It was only a matter of time
looking deeply into his eyes
That I'd realize
The *truth* of his disguise

- **High Horse** -
Rita Conestabile

A global Kaleidoscope
Lies ahead
Destinations galore
Inside my head
Trillions of colors
From sea to shore
Fulfilling the dream
I vow to explore
The people, places and things
I *so* adore

- Global Kaleidoscope -
Rita Conestabile

With the scent of magnolia on my morning ride
Under feathery white clouds
Billowing across the sky
My legs just beginning to feel the burn
With senses alive for the life that I yearn
I quell the urge to be dismayed
I'd rather dwell upon the beauty of nature displayed
The evidence of lilies that came and went
In gardens forgotten, their beauty now spent
The clock of nature set in eternal time
With angels and fairies, their beauty sublime
I'd give it my all for just a *mere* glance
In a blurred visionary moment, I can still see them dance
Morning joggers pass me by
With a nod from me, they give a wink from their eye
My destination, I eventually reach
Parking my bike, now walking the beach
At this moment in time, nothing could please me more
Than to plant my feet on this Eastern shore

- Eastern Shore -
Rita Conestabile

I kneel every morning
To let him in
To center myself
Before the day begins
To each his own
Not for me to judge
Whatever you believe
I hold no grudge

- To Each His Own -
Rita Conestabile

We are brilliantly recreated
But none of us are ever duplicated
Still
We are *one* in the same
With his cross and sacrifice now lifted
He has purchased for us
Our eternal gain

- Eternal Gain -
Rita Conestabile

Take it or leave it
It's that simple
The choice
Will *always* be yours...

- Take It or Leave It -
Rita Conestabile

She challenges the storm
He is her vicious mate
Unarmed and ready to accept her fate
Knowing that only a bolt of *lightning*
Can manifest the calm she never knew...

- The Storm -
Rita Conestabile

Recognizing it is half the battle
Believing in it is what it takes
Even when the door is shut
Love comes home and permeates its way
Through even the smallest crack in a window
Can you embrace it without keeping score?
Can you liberate your mindset
From the heartbreak you've known before?
Let it fill your room, with its heavenly perfume
Intoxicating your senses to an ultimate degree
Of a newfound you
Inhaling in love, breathes out all burdens
And those who are imprisoned are suddenly free
This is how love enters
Let's *open* the door
And let it in

- **Love Comes Home** -
Rita Conestabile

I miss you more
In so many ways
Time has outnumbered
The time of our days
I often reminisce
When time stands still
I miss you more
And I always will

- I Miss You More -
Rita Conestabile

There's a station in the sky
That glows at night
I'd see it as a child
Oft' times gazing with fright
Its ambient light so magical to me
Was it possible that *only I* could see?
With nervous excitement
Each night I'd stare
To catapult my dreams
Of someday going there
I'd keep this a secret
As we Scorpios tend to do
Waiting for just the right moment
To share this with you

- Station In The Sky -
Rita Conestabile

Swirls and twirls
Dreams and butterflies
These are the soft petal curls
Resting on the shoulders
Of my little girl

- Swirls and Twirls -
Rita Conestabile

Most deeply in love...
Most certainly was she
Exalted by one - as *brilliant* as he

- Most Deeply In Love -
Rita Conestabile

Drenched in sun
Is alright with me
let it blind the darkness
When we can't see
While others may argue
Over who is right or wrong
You and I will dance in the moonlight
To our favorite song

- Drenched In Sun -
Rita Conestabile

There in the foggy distance of eternity
It stood
A pyramid it seemed
A fortress of *impenetrable* insolence
Yet always accessible and present in her dreams
From there she could hear the ringing
Of the somber tenor bells
Coming from Westminster Abbey
Tolling repeatedly on the hour
Silhouetted against the shadows
Of a dark and dreary English sky
A mecca for Poets
With their *exhausting* attempts
To delegate just the right words
To rapture the audience standing before them
But sadly, once spoken, they too will dissipate
Like tears flowing from our eyes
Alas, *all the world's a stage*
Especially inside the mind of the author
Desperately seeking an exit
For his words
Trapped inside, this imaginary maze

- All the World's A Stage -
Rita Conestabile

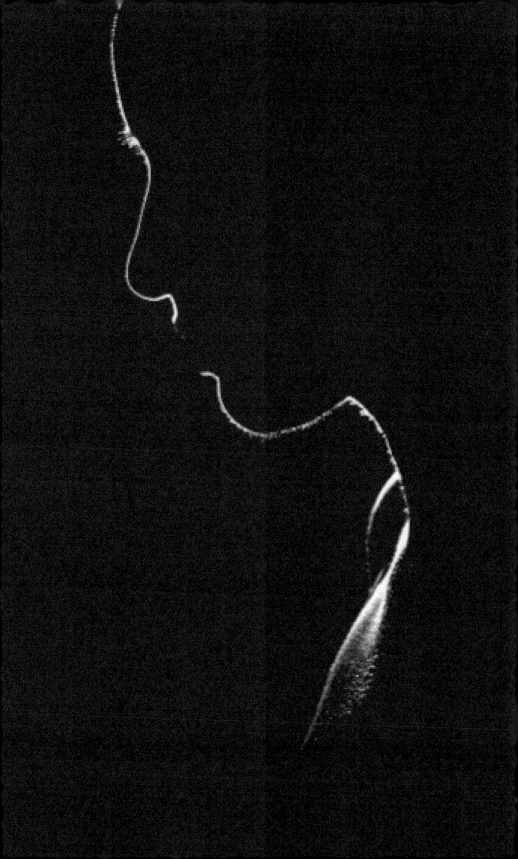

Always alluring
With a subliminal glow
Cleverly concealing
The wounds of her woes
Still shrouded in mystery
Her heart doesn't stray
Loyalty in abundance
Is the scorpion way

- The Scorpion Way -
Rita Conestabile

If not for you
Who would I be?
Our paths have crossed
Generations of seas
Without the sorrow of life's inevitable pain
How could we measure the gratitude we gain?
What is the worth of having it all
If in my abundance I witness your fall?
We move forward in friction, when attempting to erase
The facts of history, we just can't replace
Leave it alone – can't you see?
If not for you, who would I be?

- If Not For You -
Rita Conestabile

I've set my sights
On living the mundane
Sealing the cracks
Where teardrops rain
I've settled my thoughts
On clear blue skies
To love this life
As the years roll by

- Living the Mundane -
Rita Conestabile

She was wired to be
A contemplative
Sometimes philosophical
Thinker
Not by *choice*
But by nature
With endless thoughts
Blowing in the wind
She was wild and free
As deep as the sea
Roaming aimlessly
With insatiable curiosity
That girl always has been
And always will be, *me*

- Wild and Free -
Rita Conestabile

You are my world
My life
My dream
No and, Ifs, or buts...
And *nothing*
In between

- Nothing In Between -
Rita Conestabile

How more intimate
Can you get
Than to be *inside*
Another person's head?
Once you're there
The responsibility is enormous

- Two In One -
Rita Conestabile

Words can harden and blister
With all his might
He tries to forget her
With an obscene version
Of fairy tale blue
Shoved down her throat
By someone she thought she knew
It's never pretty
On the other side of
It's too Late
Because this shade of blue
Always turns
love into hate

- It's Too Late -
Rita Conestabile

The very essence
Of me
Has always been
You...

- Essence -
Rita Conestabile

The love we had
Created an eternity
That remains
Even if
You love someone else
It'll *never* be the same

- Never Be The Same -
Rita Conestabile

Too young, so tough
I'll never forget her bright baby blues
Such devastating words, shattered hope
Came crashing down on you
Being with you that day
Left me feeling helpless too
But I promised
To walk each step with you
Dearest Kelly, on this day you were born
Throughout your life, a warriors strength was shown
You were such a blessing
Your pain and suffering is now through
May God's eternal light, shine brilliantly on you...

- Birthday Poem for Kelly -
Rita Conestabile

Our faith
So often tested
Our soul's reliance
Through Christ manifested
Eventually
We will all be as one
Together with the Holy Spirit
The Father and The Son

- **Christ Manifested** -
Rita Conestabile

With tremendous dread
I do fear
The night the moon
Does not appear
For in its glory
My heart takes flight
lighting the way
Through my darkest night

- With **Tremendous Dread** -
Rita Conestabile

You'll only suffer
Trying to sabotage me
Get yourself *together*
And set yourself free

- Get Yourself Together -
Rita Conestabile

The peace of love
Rest's quietly inside your heart
Let it drown out the noise
Of injustice and hatred
That tears this world apart
Build on the humanity
That each of us share
Alone or united
Show someone in need
How much you care

- The Peace of Love -
Rita Conestabile

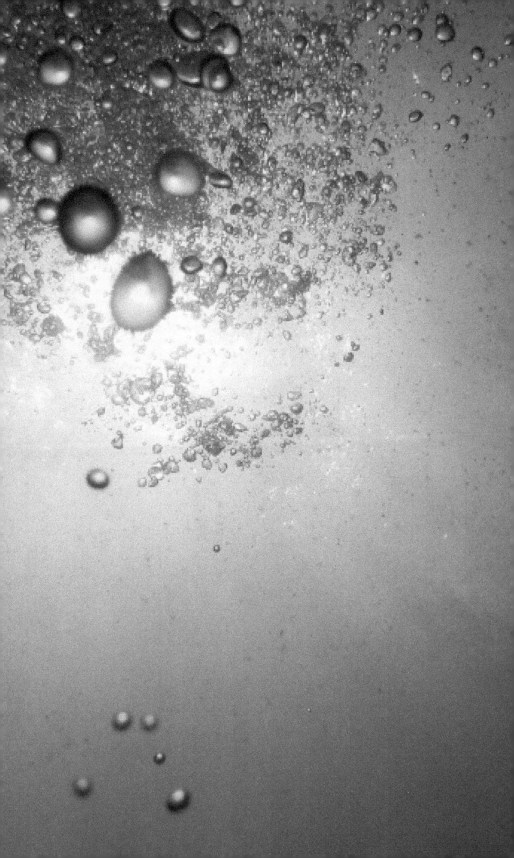

One of the greatest
Gifts
We can give each other
Is the *confidence* to fail
Without being made to *feel*
Like a failure

- The Confidence to Fail -
Rita Conestabile

I love you through and through
I love
Everything you do
I'll love you forever
And *then...*
I'll love you all over again

- Forever and Then -
Rita Conestabile

What *could've* been
Wasn't meant to be...
Let it go
And be at peace

- Let It Go -
Rita Conestabile

A kindred spirit
I seek to find
To embrace God's beauty
And enlighten my mind
To have and to hold
To love and to know
That the *promise* of love
Will continue to grow

- A Kindred Spirit I Seek To Find -
Rita Conestabile

I came back for you
A thousand years have passed
But I made it through
No longer do I yearn
For days gone by
Since death's lesson
I must learn
The sea holds the key
To return you to me
Spirits of ages
Wash along her eternal shore
Listen my love, 'tis you - that I adore
Come find me
And leave me nevermore

- Spirits of Ages -
Rita Conestabile

Be the voice of reason
You so long to hear
Embrace the unknown
Be at peace with your fears
The power you possess
Outweighs all the above
Your weapon of choice
Should always be *love*...

- Weapon of Choice -
Rita Conestabile

I am thoroughly saturated
In love with the sea
I send her a whisper
She roars back at me
Not to be rude
But to let it be known
That Love is ferocious
With its depth unknown

- Thoroughly Saturated -
Rita Conestabile

The jurisdiction of honor
Has been thoroughly bled
Every devious action
Breeds malicious words
So often said
Catastrophic, are the tendencies
When intentions are to abolish
Truths creed
This is the ultimate slavery
That no man can free
Stripped of all armor
In this war against love
We must
Plant the seeds of forgiveness
And pray to God above

- The Jurisdiction of Honor -
Rita Conestabile

These booties made with love
Have traveled through time
And across the miles
To touch the hearts
Of the babies who wear them
And for their parents
To bring a smile
We recall the memory and the legacy
Of those gone before
Like these booties
Made by your great - grandmother Romana
Whose love for you
And our family
Will live *forever* more

- For Marcus: Booties -
Rita Conestabile

Obscure and unknown
She was the rose
That preceded the thorn
Forever wild
In my heart she'll stay
Her spirit alive
'Till my dying day

- The Rose -
Rita Conestabile

Darkness creeps in
Even on the brightest day
Teardrops form
Shaped out of pain
Under a moonlit sky
In the pouring rain
Torrential is their downfall
To cleanse us one and all
While angel guardians of the heart
Keep the demons
From tearing us apart

- Darkness -
Rita Conestabile

Things that curve
And come back around
In so deep
turned upside down
Love letters and this number
Always significant as I recall
like wings out of nowhere
Before a big fall
The great 28 with 14 in between
My mate in fate
Throughout my life it seems
To remind me
That the way it is
Was always meant to be

- 28 -
Rita Conestabile

Significantly imperfect
Amongst the rarest of ones
The journey
Of this Ravishing Pearl
Has only just begun...

- Significantly Imperfect -
Rita Conestabile

About the Author

Ravishing Pearl is author Rita Conestabile's first published book of poetry. She was born in Southern Italy, grew up in upstate New York, and for many years lived in New York City pursuing a career in music. A writer, poet, muse, singer, songwriter, and lyricist presently residing in the seaside town of Ocean City, Maryland. She is the proud mother of three grown, successful children, and during 2020's global pandemic, became a "Nonna" with the arrival of her firstborn grandchild. Rita has enjoyed creative writing since early childhood and is inspired by all aspects of art, nature, music and life, with a passionate desire for living it to the fullest!